100 ROOMS

MANY UNTOLD PARABLES OF THE EMPTY ROOM

"The idea of the future, pregnant with an infinity of possibilities, is more fruitful than the future itself, and this is why we find more charm in hope than in possession, in dreams than in reality."

_ Henri Bergson

TABLE OF CONTENTS

100 Rooms

The entire world was like a palace with countless rooms whose doors opened into one another. We were able to pass from one room to the next only by exercising our memories and imaginations, but most of us, in our laziness, rarely exercised these capacities, and forever remained in the same room.

Orhan Pamuk

PROLOGUE

As a sequel to *The Empty Room: Fragmented Thoughts on Space* (2020), this book elaborates the same theme with one hundred iterations of a square room, each of which tells a different story of the emptiness between the walls.

The Empty Room, in the absence of any visual materials, was composed of poems, aphorisms, and a collection of quotes portraying the room and the emptiness as the essence of architecture. Now, in the following pages, 100 square rooms complement many blurry images of the empty room with a visual guide. Each page consists of a plan and a physical model of a room, which is an excavation of geometry and order inherent within a square. It holds no design intention – no scale or function – but simply one of infinite possibilities that emerge from a square. This framework implies that a formal expression of a room should come from within, not from the walls that enclose the space. With these visual references, one can begin to imagine many approximations to the empty room. A line on a paper is always less, as Kahn says, but through these measurable means, the immeasurable idea of the empty room will take form in one's mind.

SEEING WITH CLOSED EYES

When I close my eyes, I recollect or dream. But when I open my eyes, all I see is now. With my eyes closed, I depart from now and somehow become time itself. I stand halfway between reality and unreality. Depending on which direction I take, I look at either the past in retrospection or the future in anticipation. With my eyes open, I see an image of the world, flattened for my retina and other senses, which is full of lies. It is only when I close my eyes that I begin to feel and understand how the past is clothed in the future, how the future is clothed in the past, how everything is continuous and simultaneous, how enormous the world and my being are. Time becomes timelessness, the measurable becomes the immeasurable, all things become one.

The immeasurable quality of something comes from what you cannot see or touch or hear or smell (or even taste). The empty room is an idea of an ideal room, which inspires you, motivates you, consoles you, warms you, speaks with you, sings for you, cries for you, loves you, and eventually becomes you. It is a room that fits differently in each person's heart but exists singularly at the same time. 100 Rooms is my personal exploration of the empty room that is in my heart, in the belief that it can also resonate with other people. Their floor plans are like closed eyes, drawn without scale or function or any purpose whatsoever. They leave the final decisions to you, my dear readers, concerning how to build it, how to enter it, how to occupy it, how to depart from it, how to return to it, how to stay in it, how to pray in it, how to play in it, and how not to do any of these at all. Through this incompleteness, they recall both ancient ruins and constructions at job sites.

In the end, the empty room is not an architectural concept. It is the feeling for the eternal and absolute being, which penetrates and fulfills our imperfect and fragile subjectivities. Creating these 100 rooms, I have assumed my role not just as an architect but rather as an archaeologist, who excavates ancient ruins and rediscovers the history of humanity; a psychologist, who taps into the subconsciousness, the mind, and the memories; a monk, who believes in his answers humbly and quietly and dedicates his whole life towards the truth; a novelist, who, finishing a new book, secretly entertains many finales for it; a prophet, who predicts destinies and offers wisdom and insights to the world.

The empty room is a room that is impossible yet always present, where long ago, now, and what lies ahead are one and the same.

100 ROOMS

I am many rooms.

RZLBD

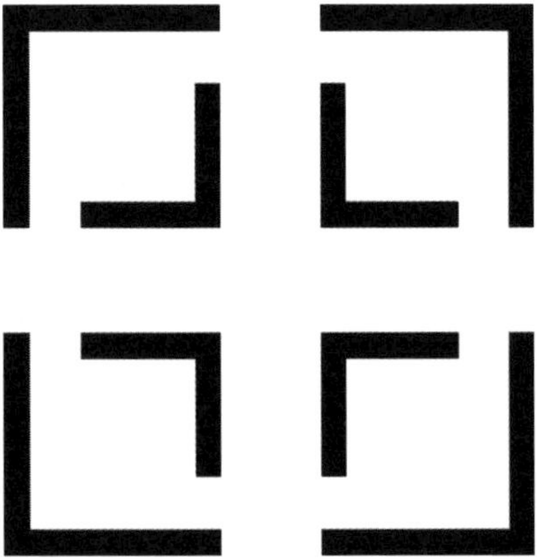

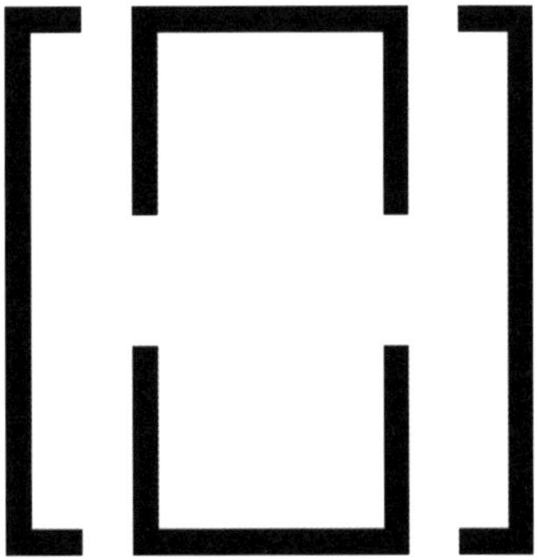

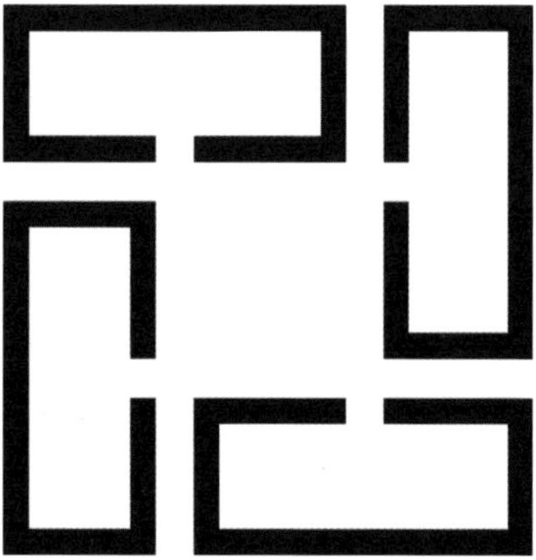

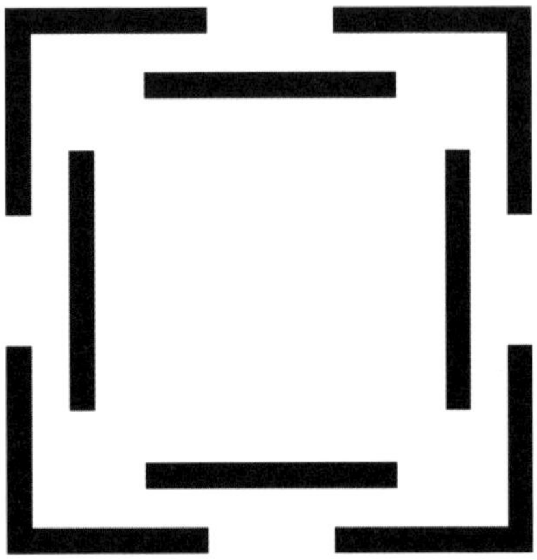

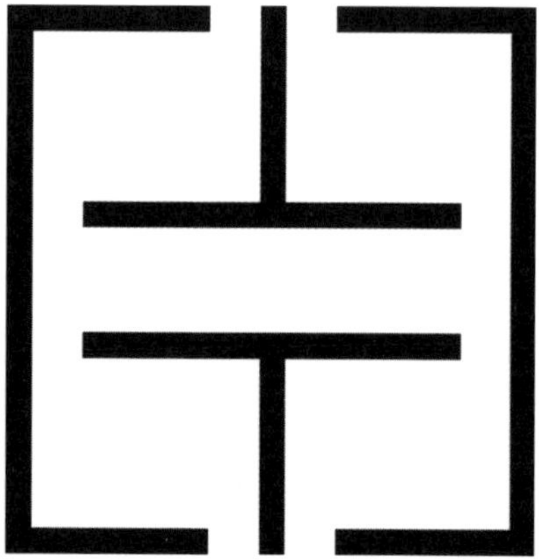

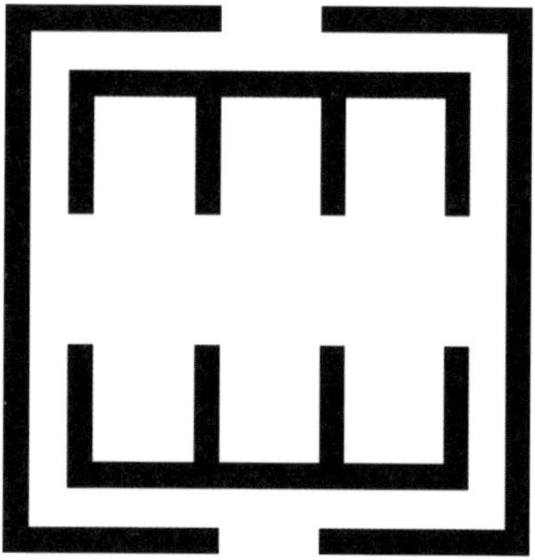

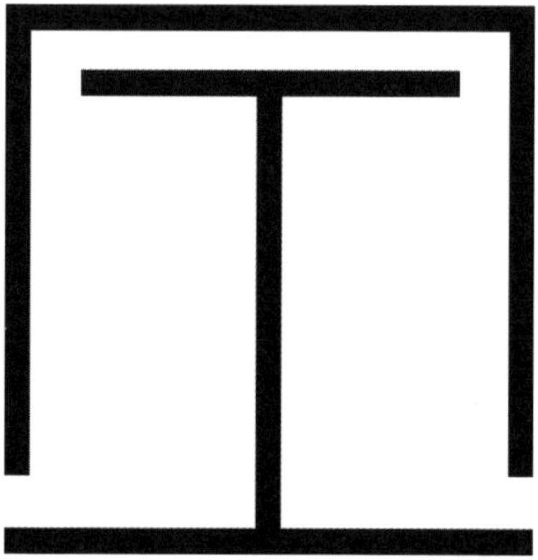

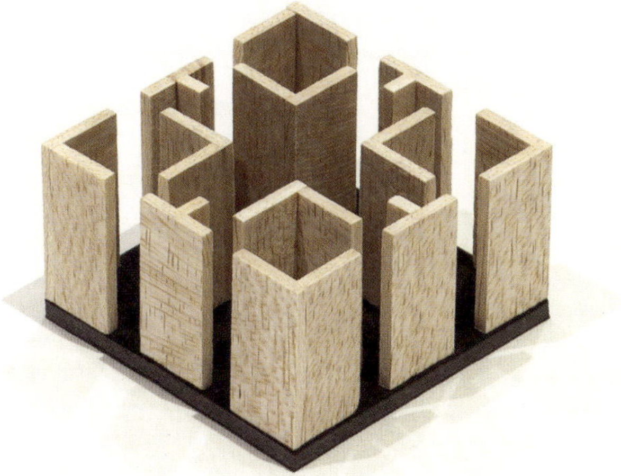

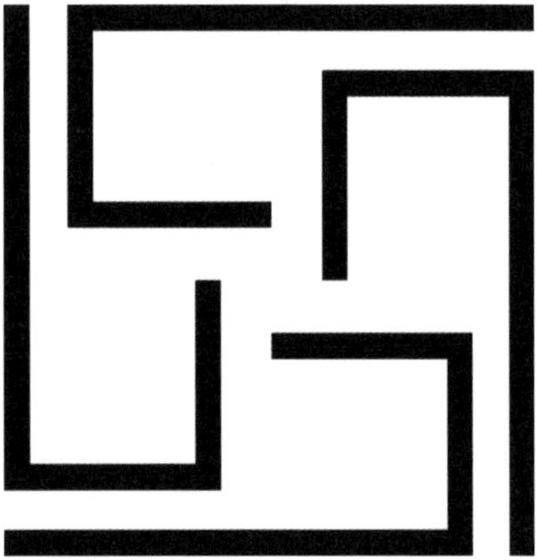

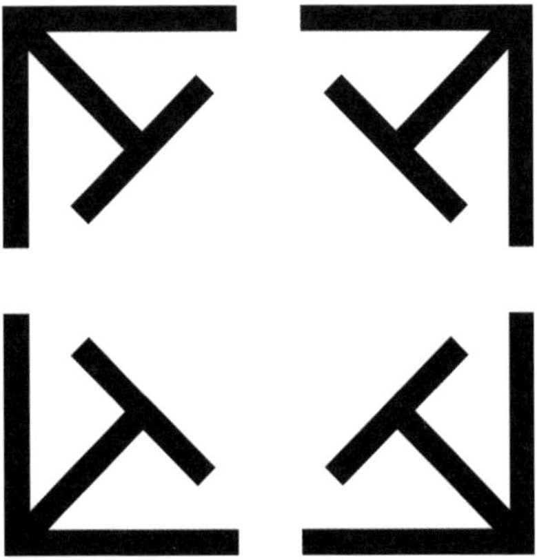

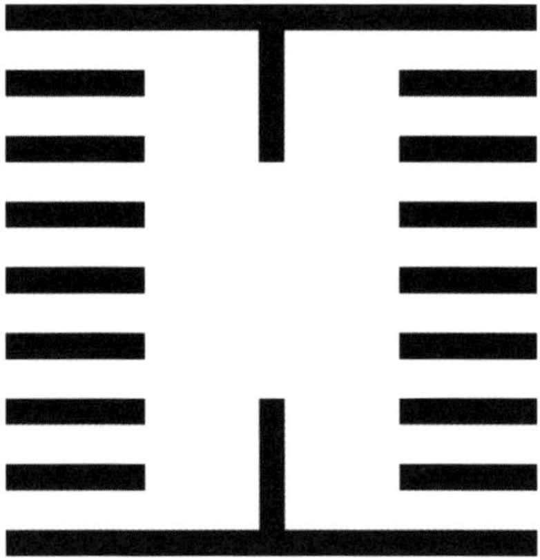

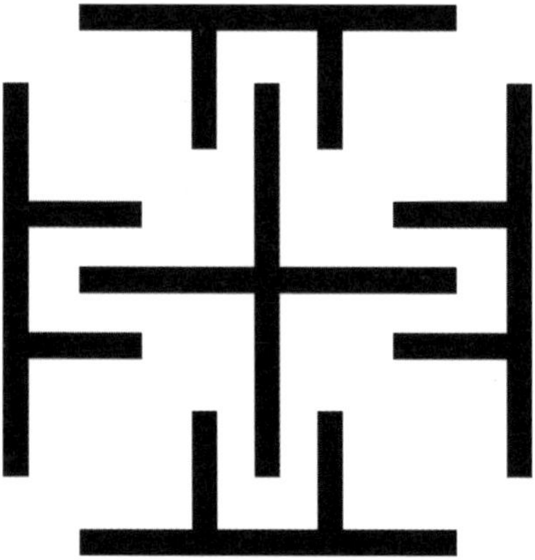

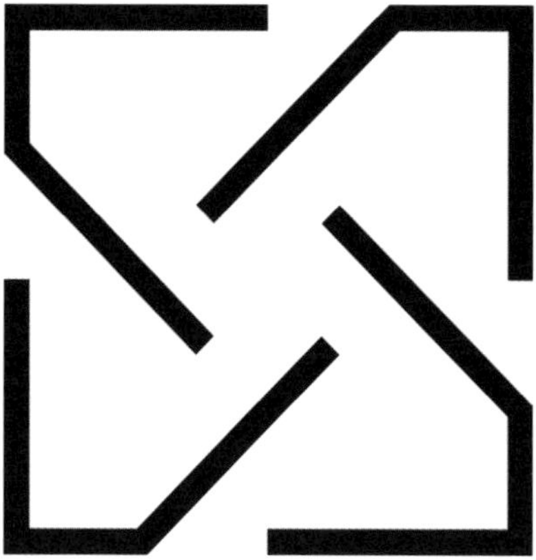

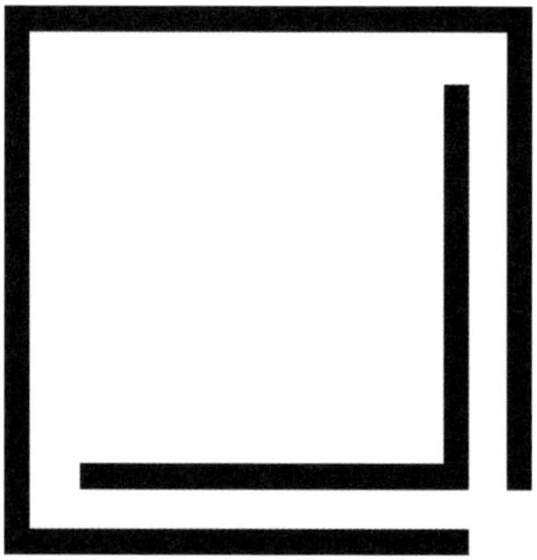

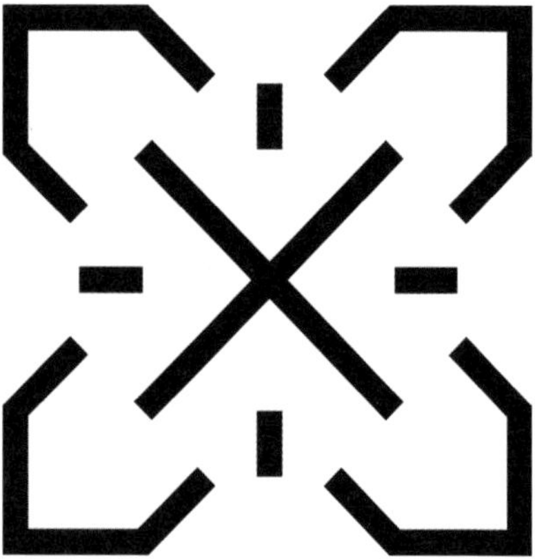

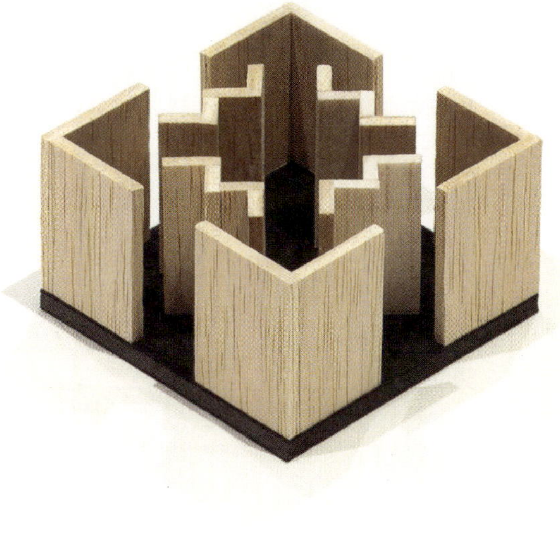

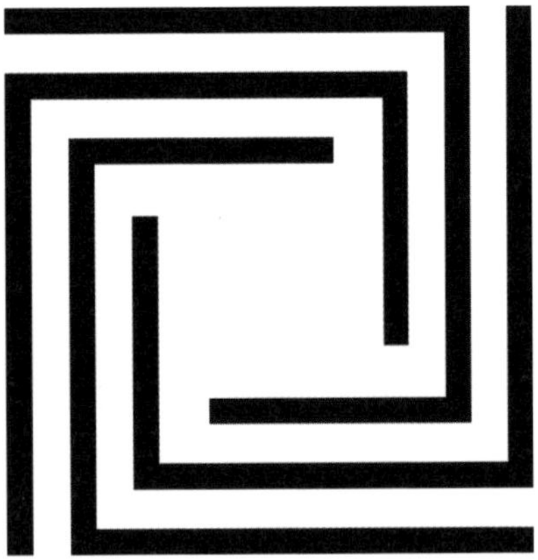

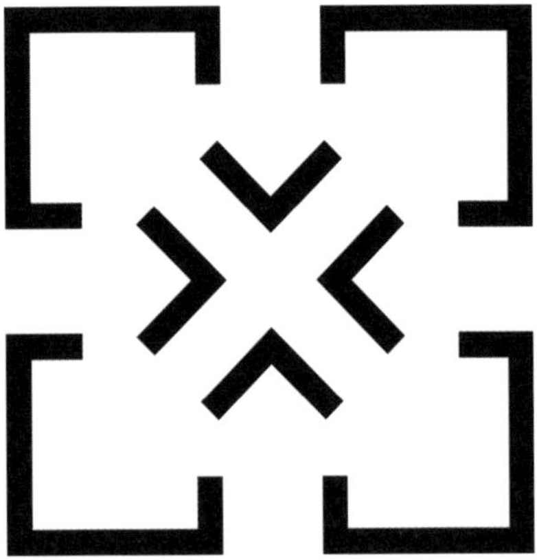

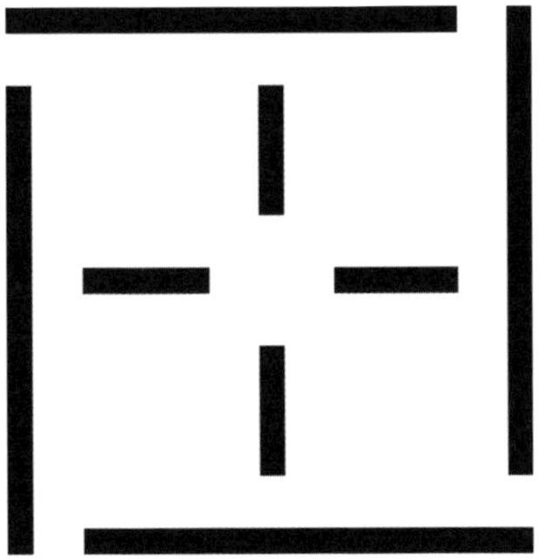

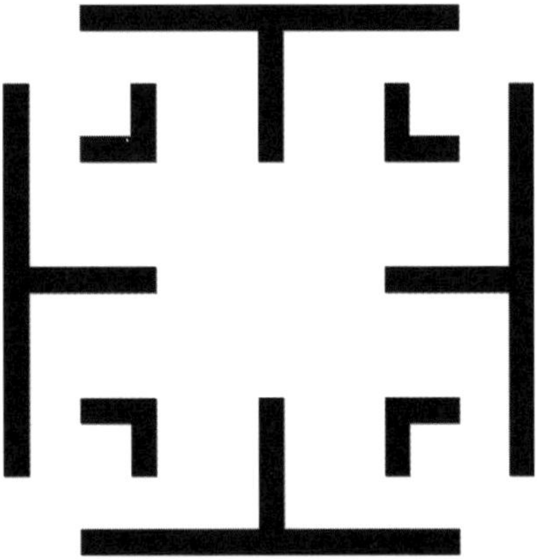

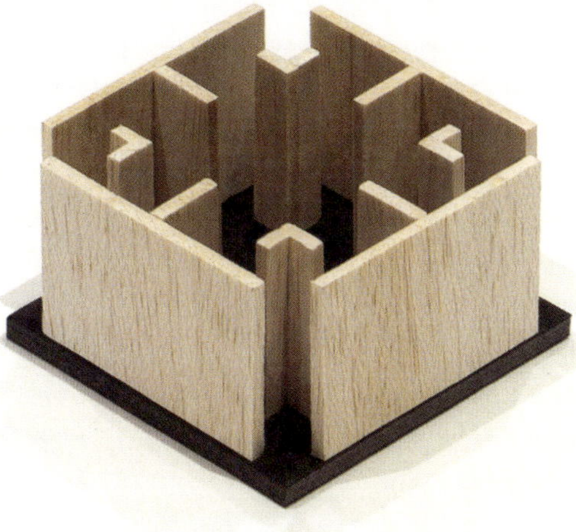

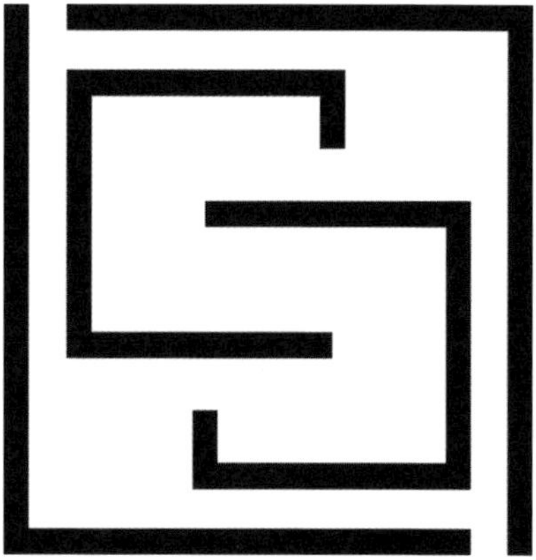

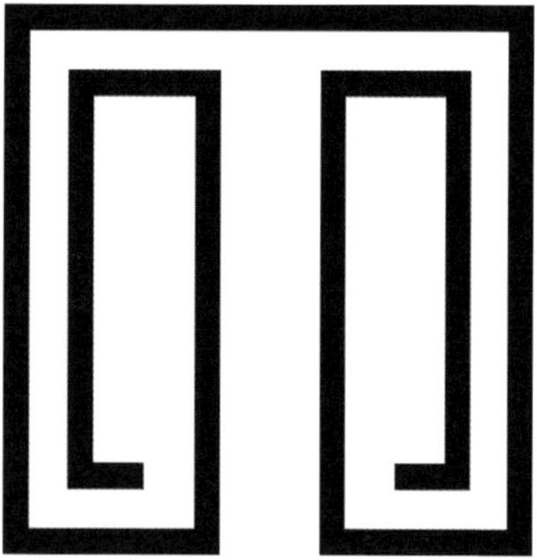

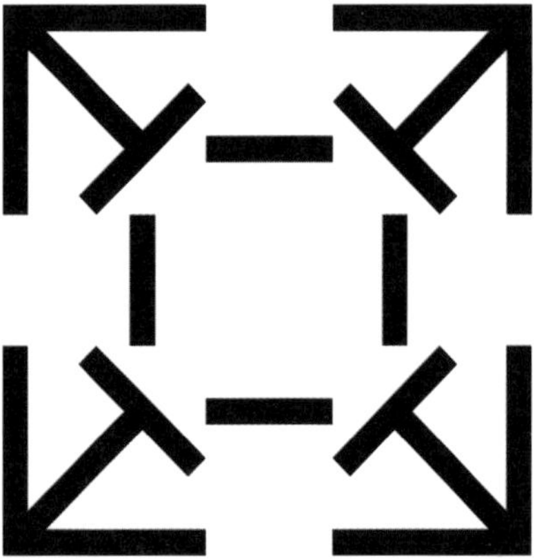

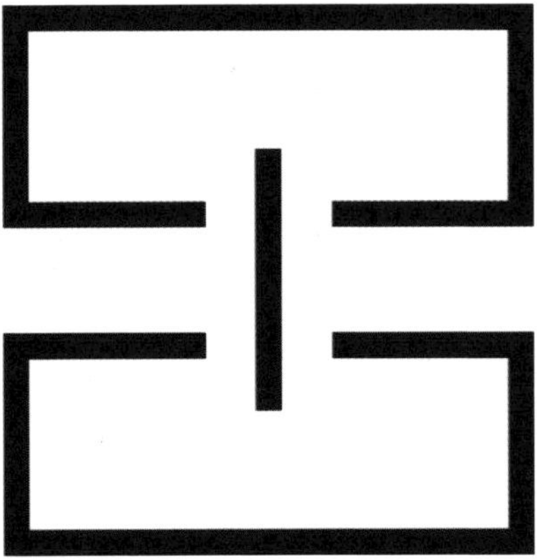

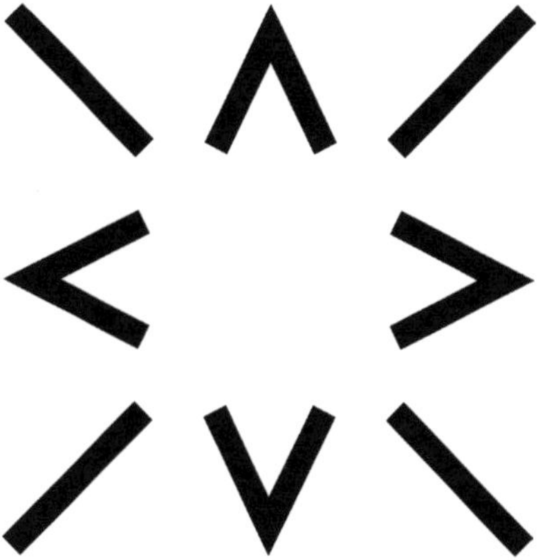

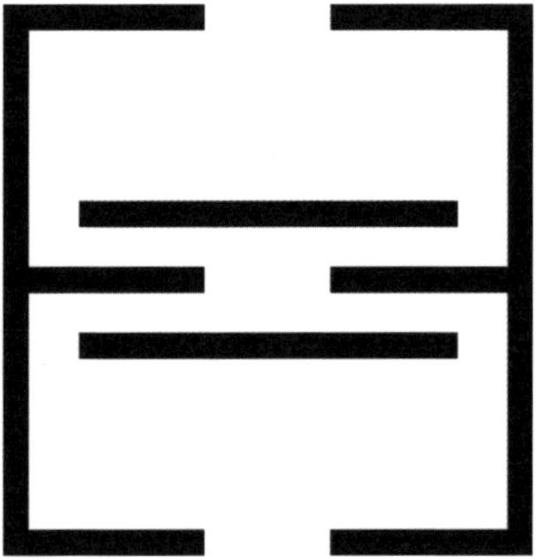

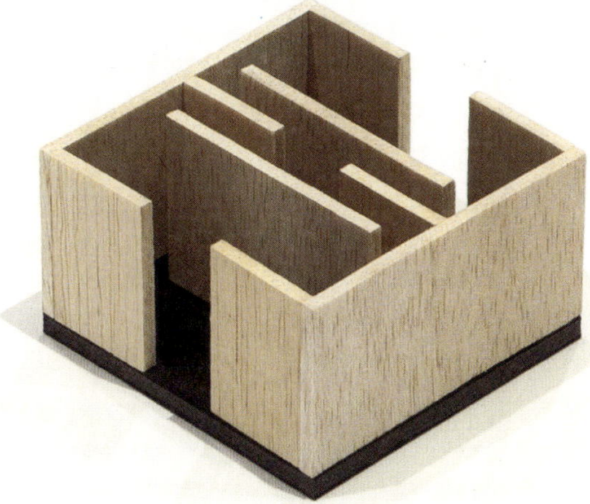

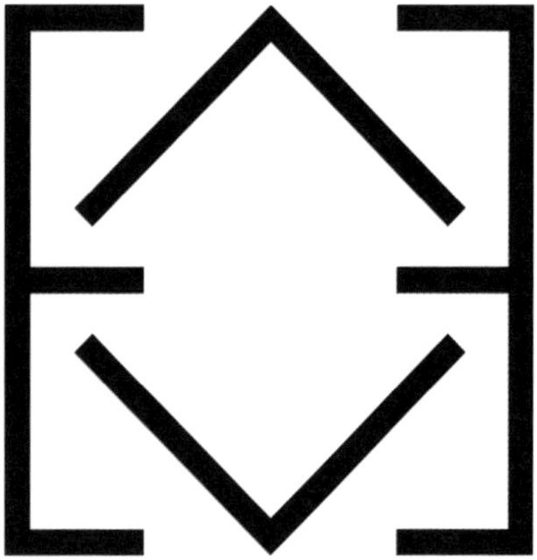

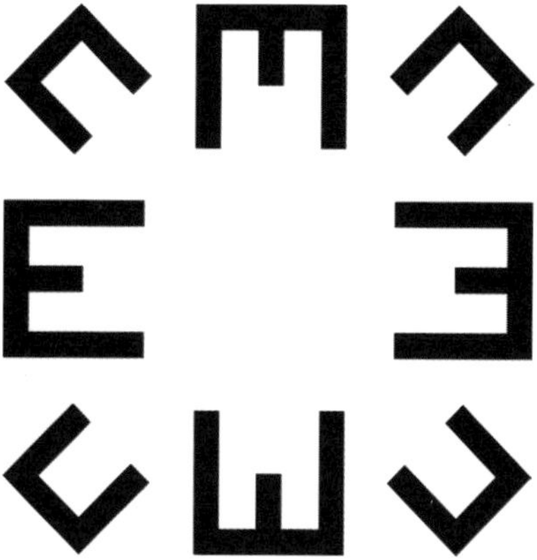

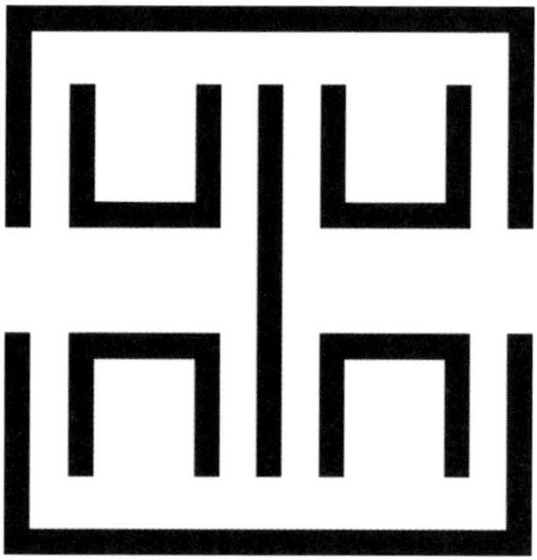

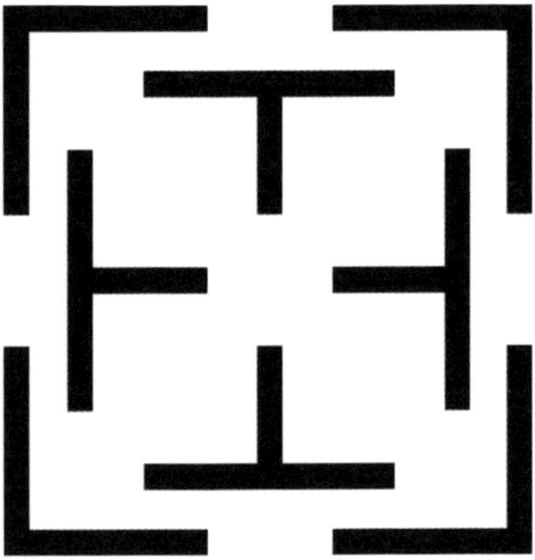

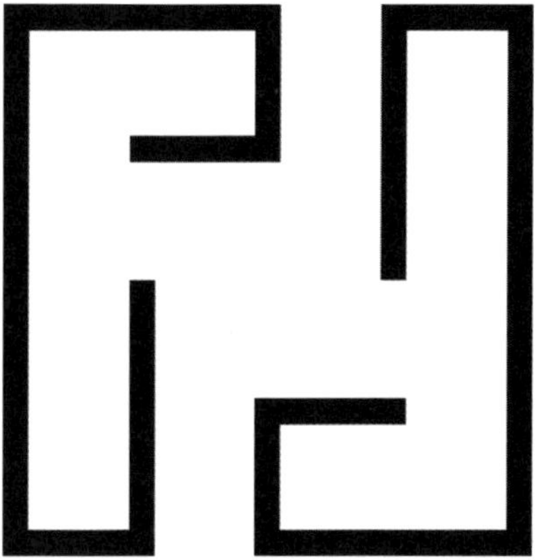

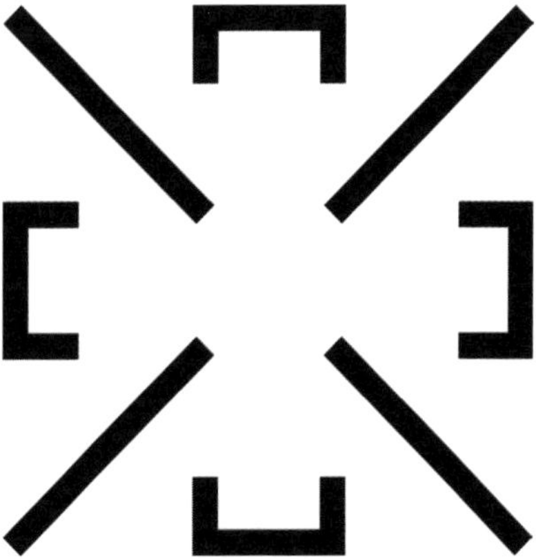

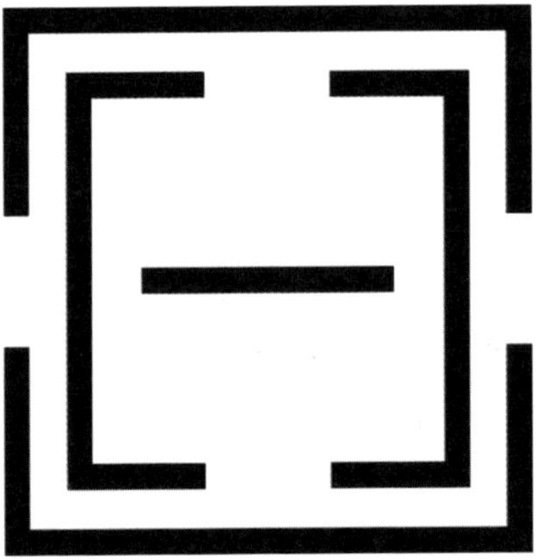

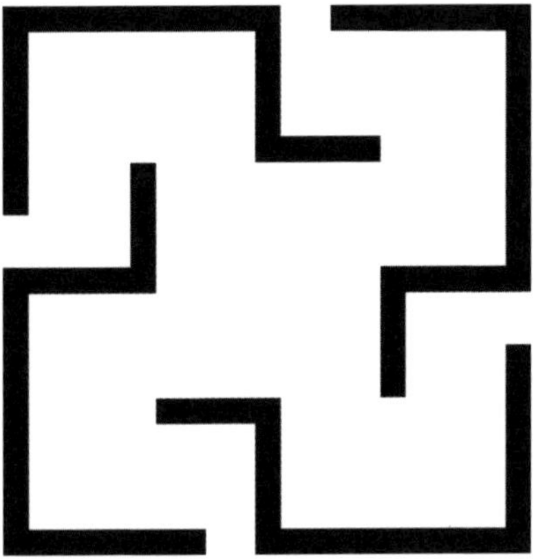

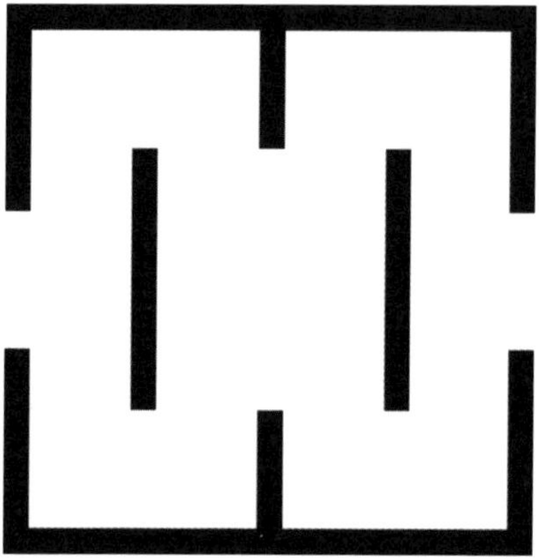

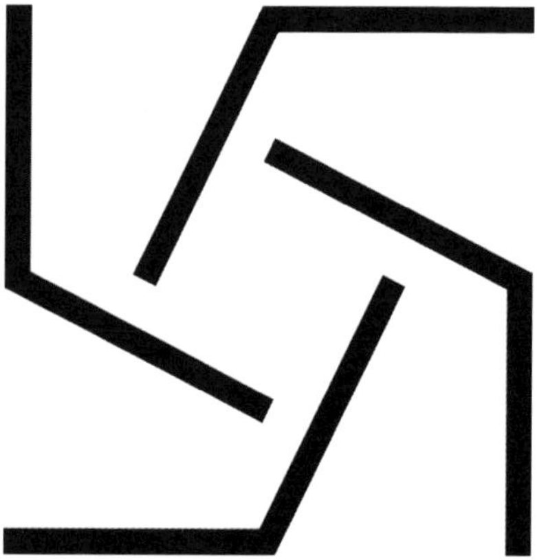

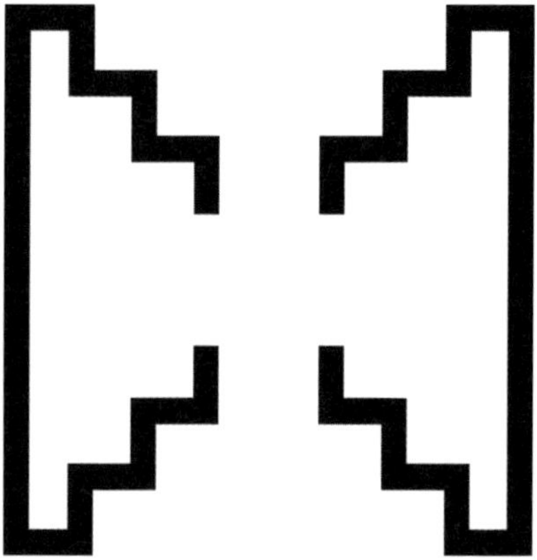

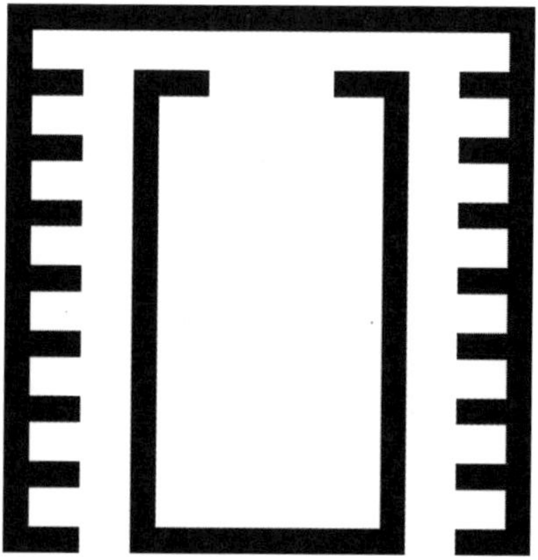

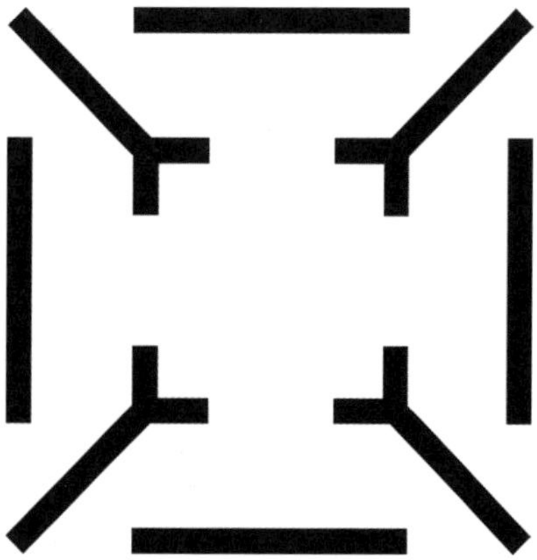

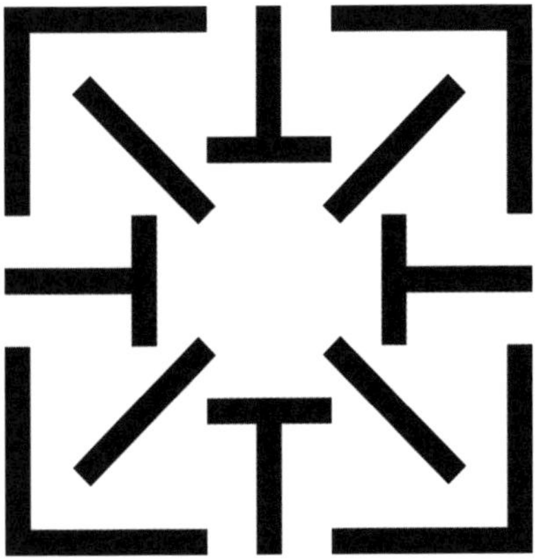

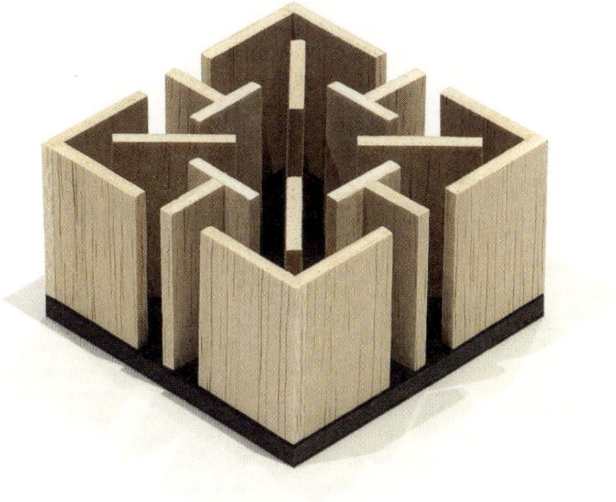

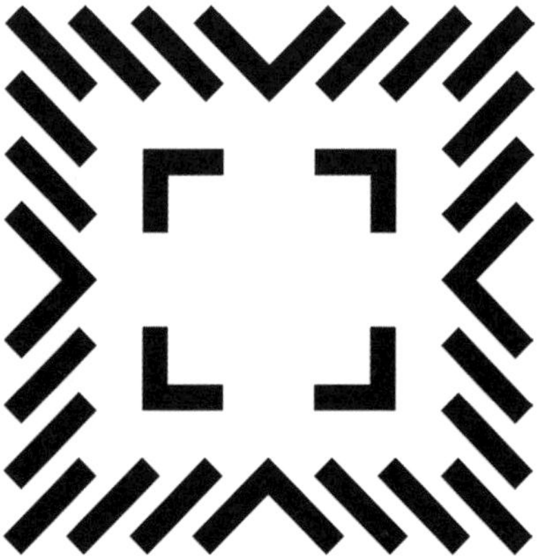

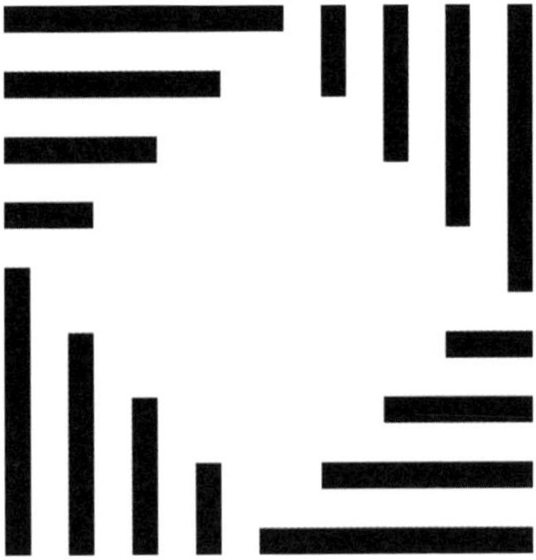

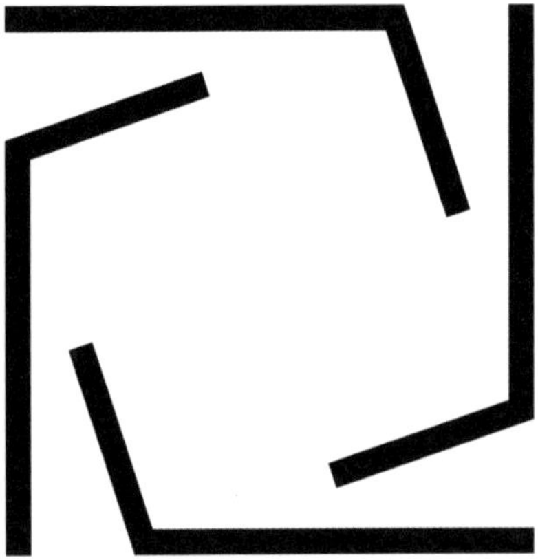

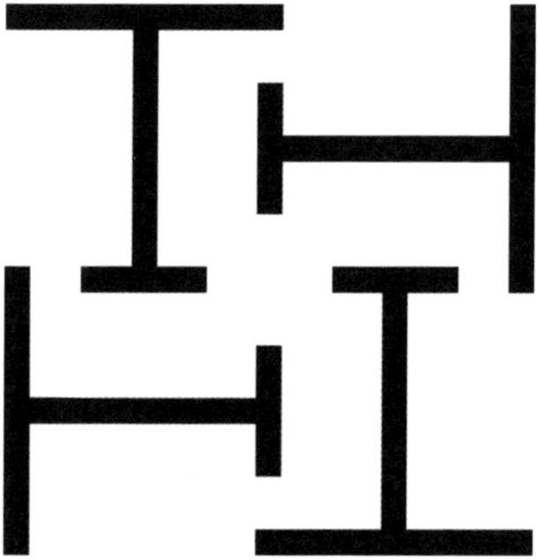

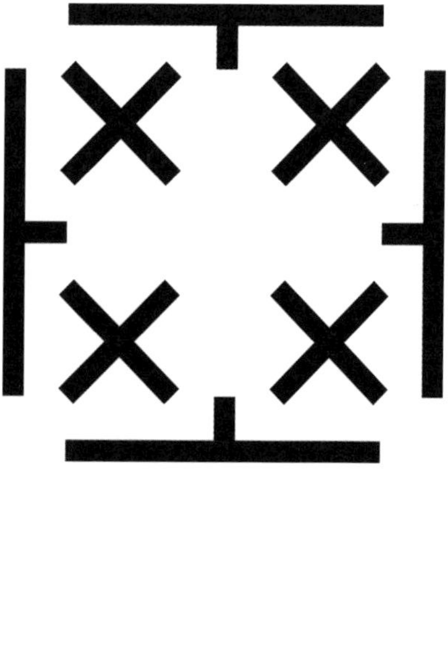

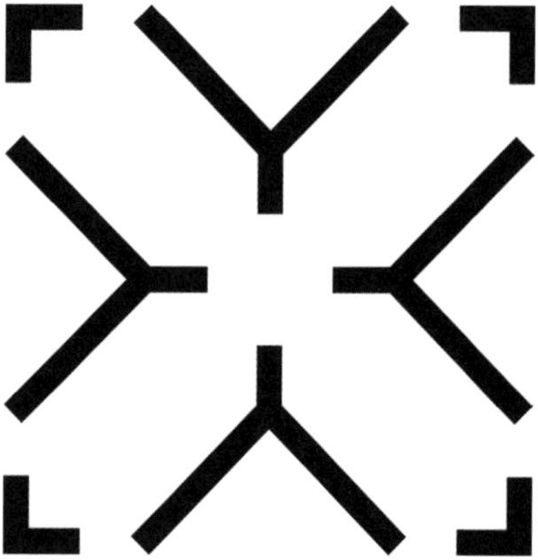

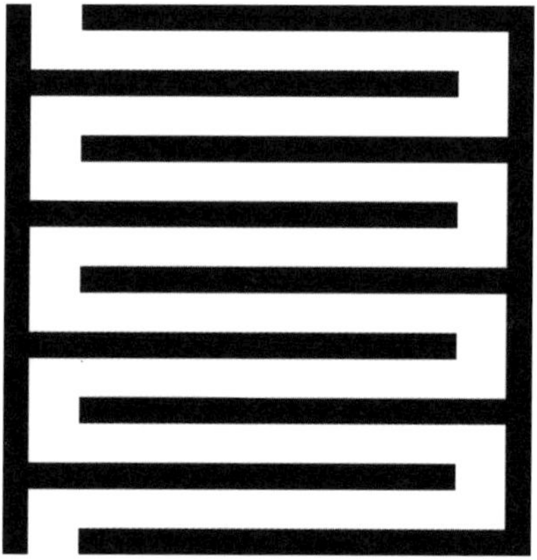

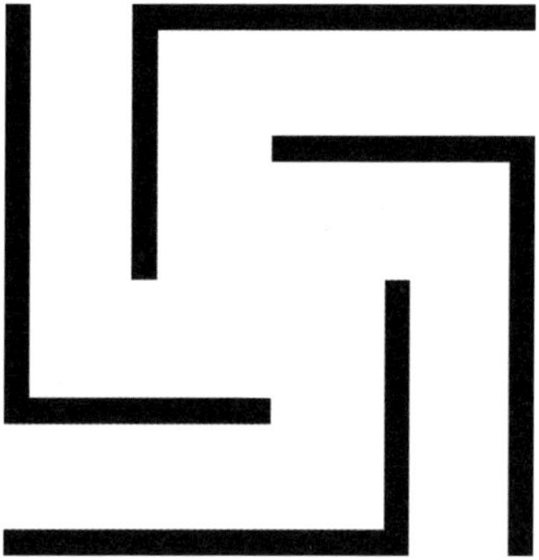

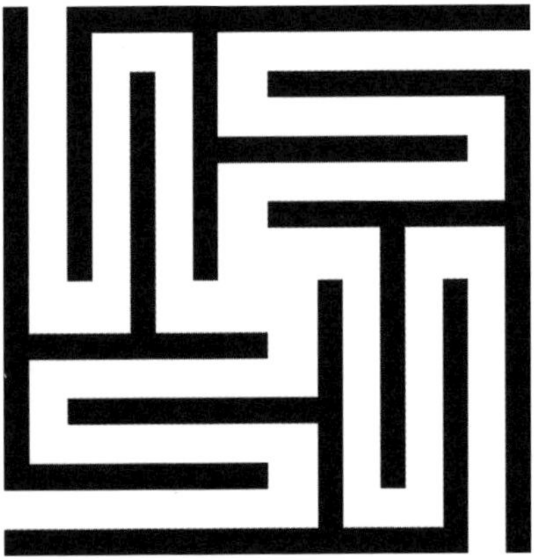

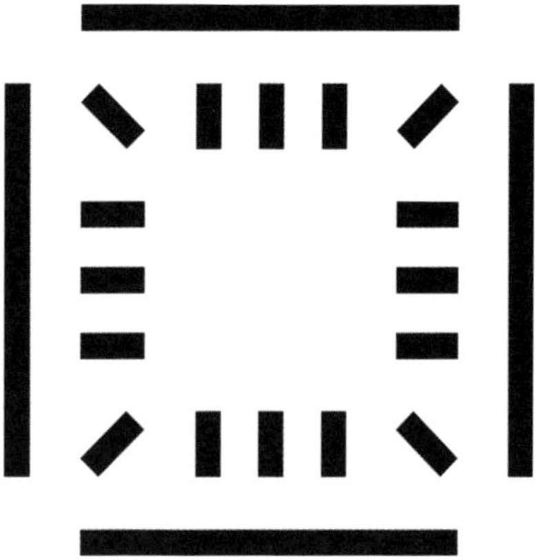

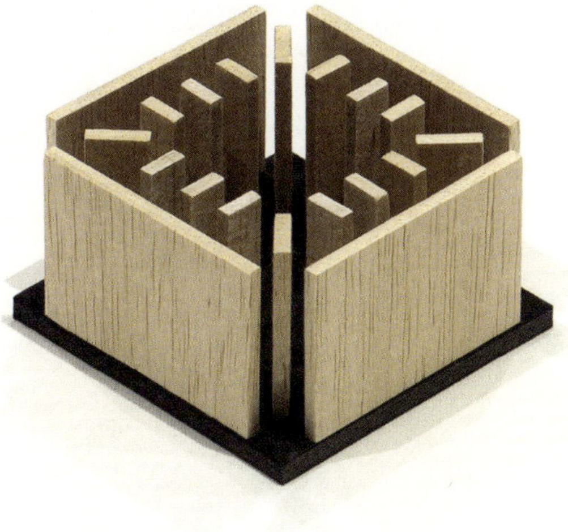

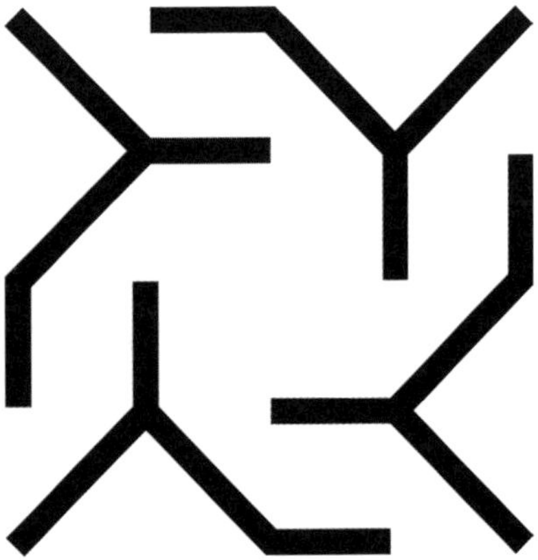

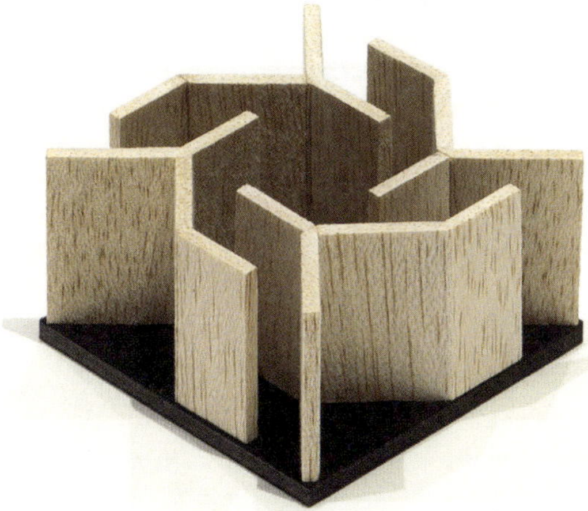

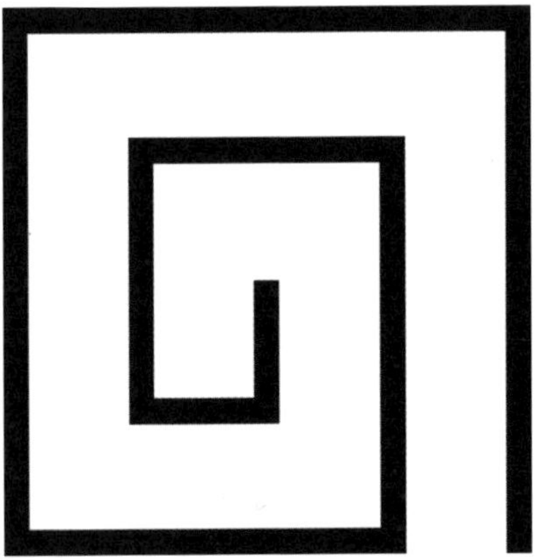

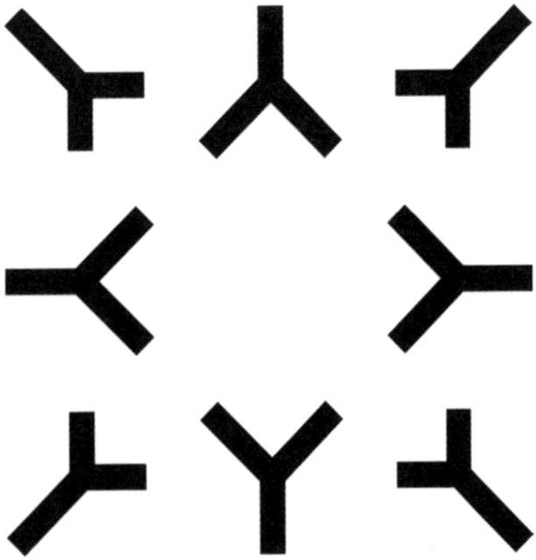

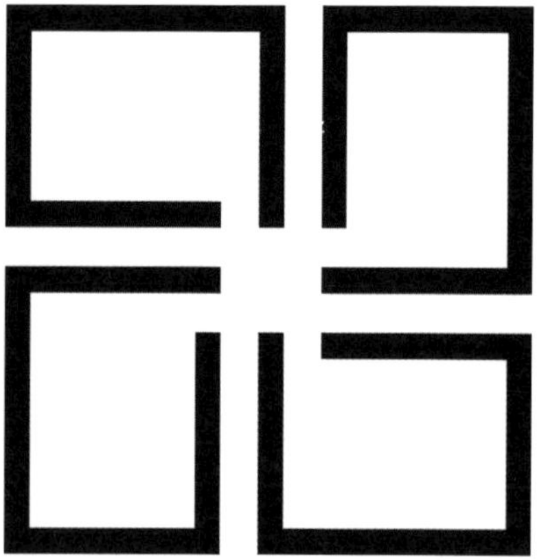

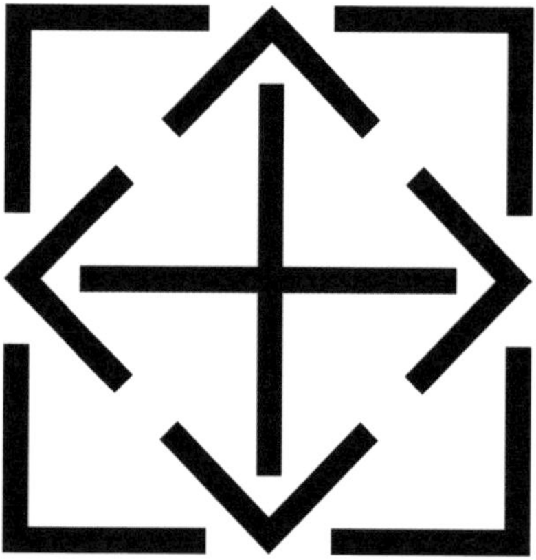

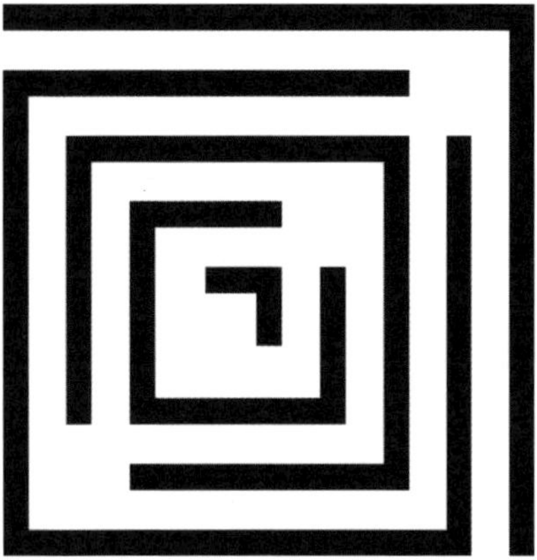

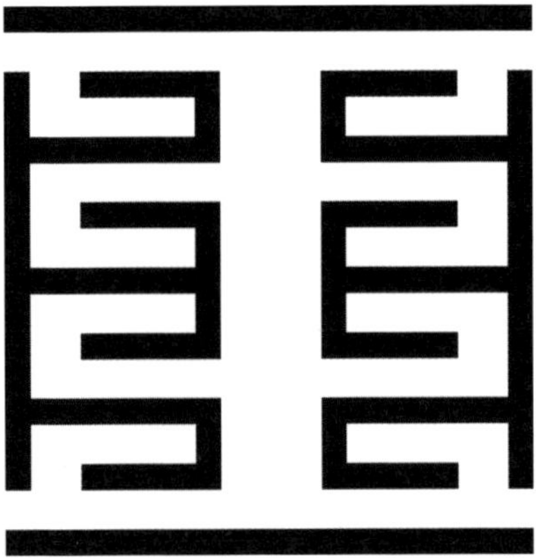

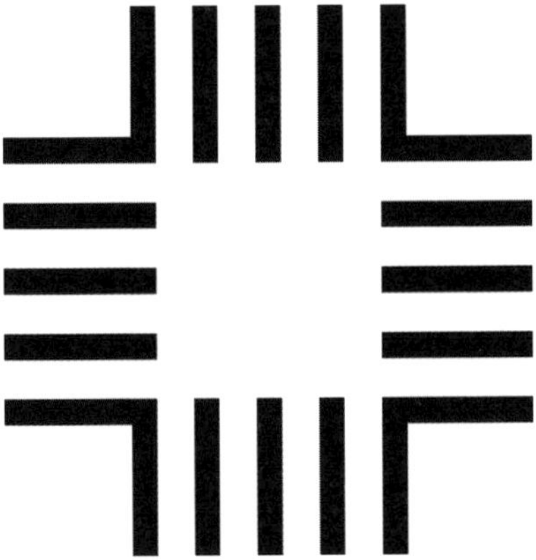

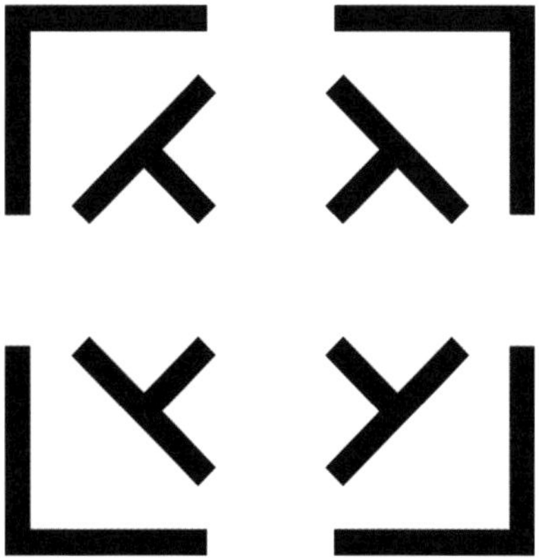

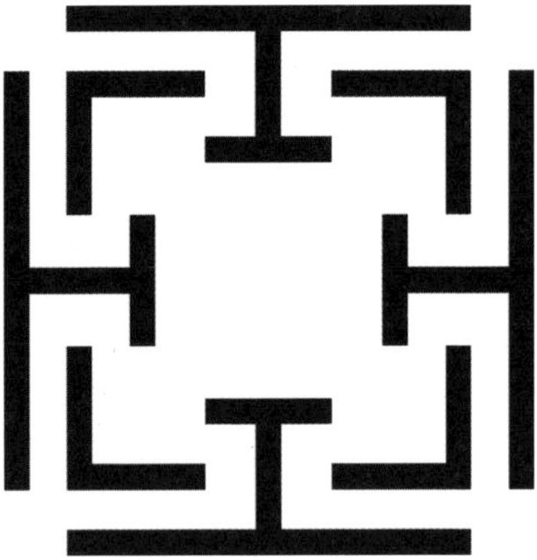

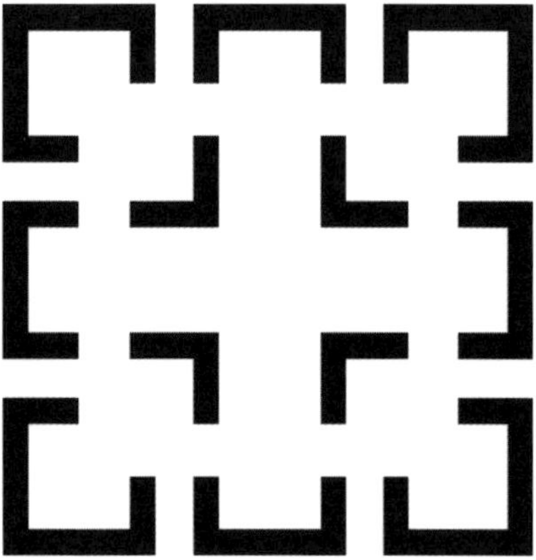

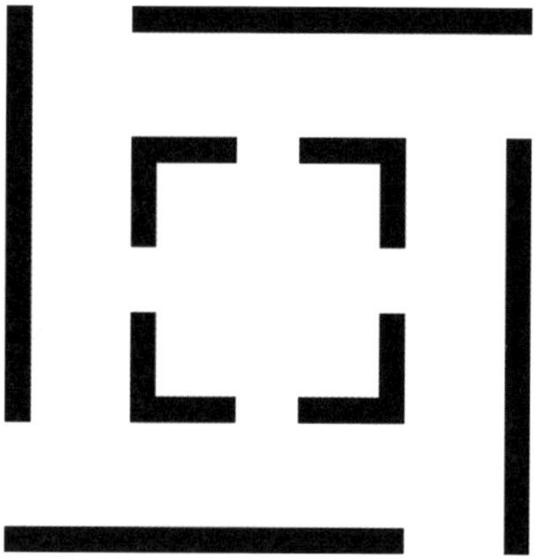

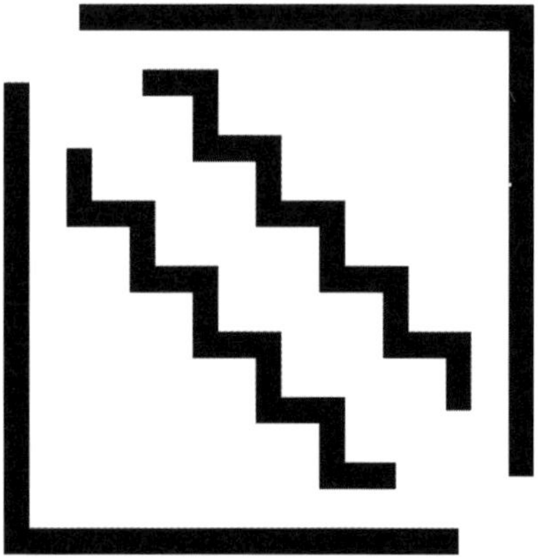

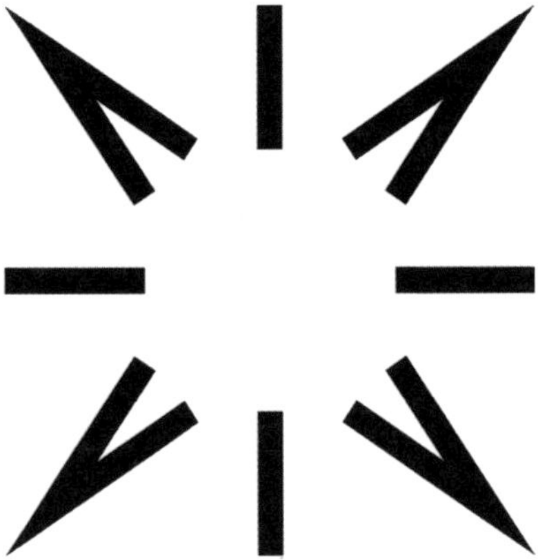

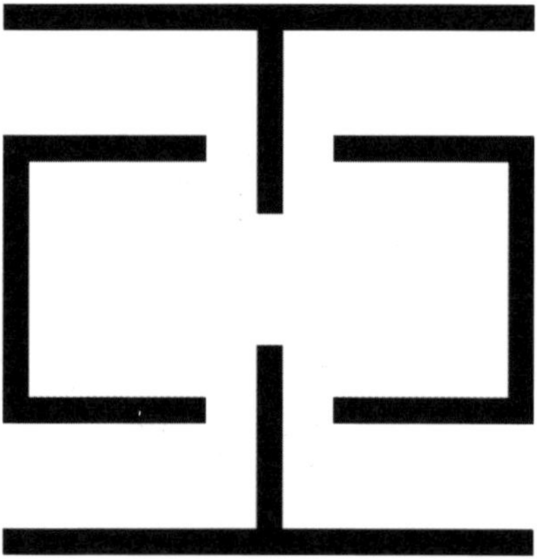

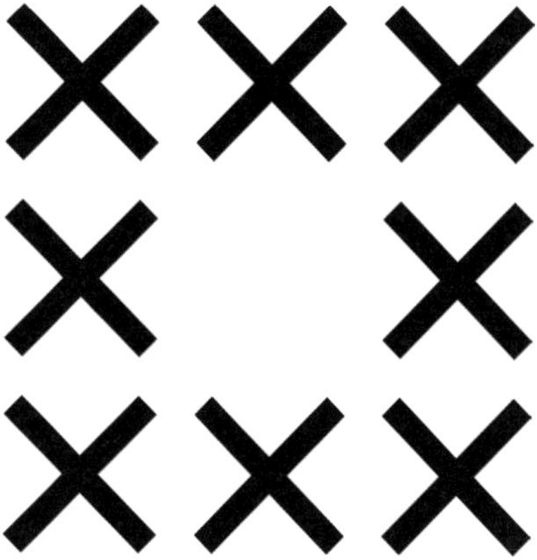

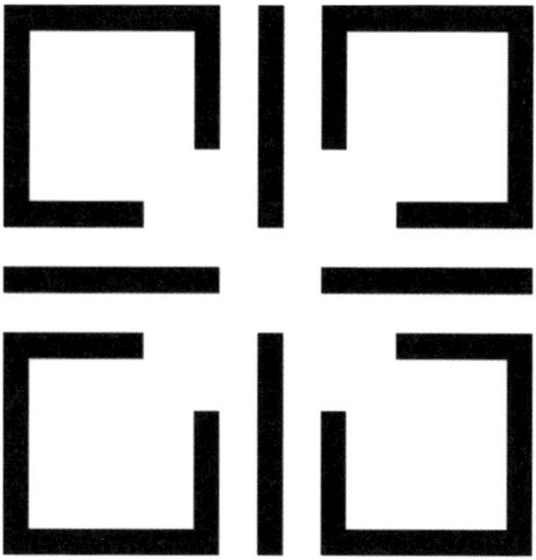

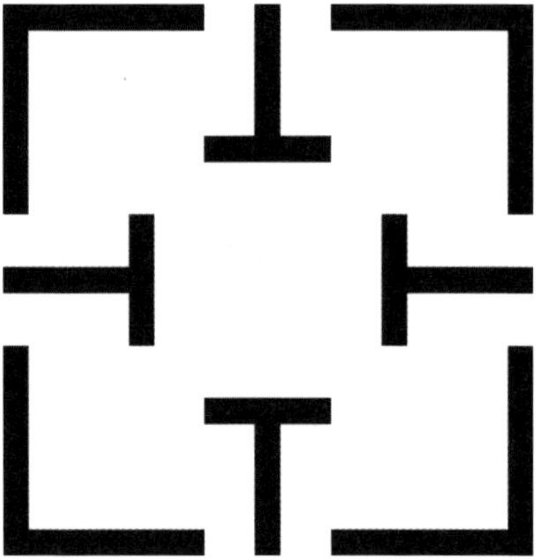

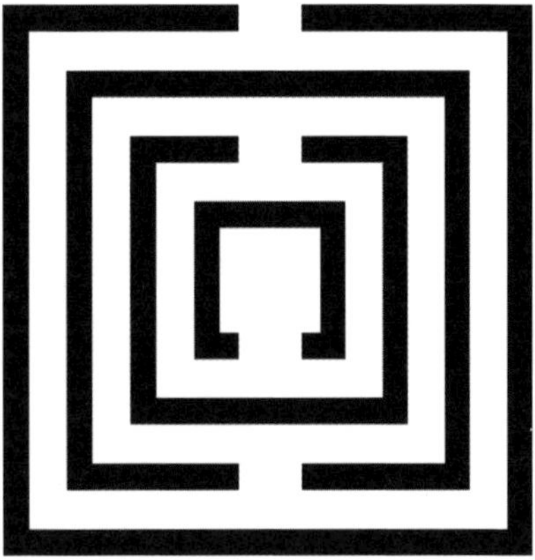

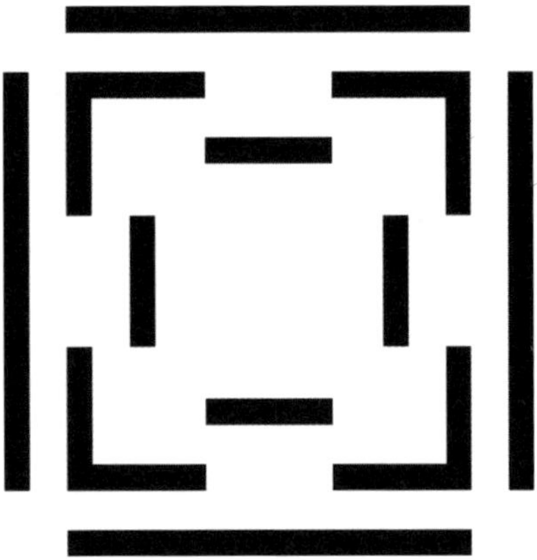

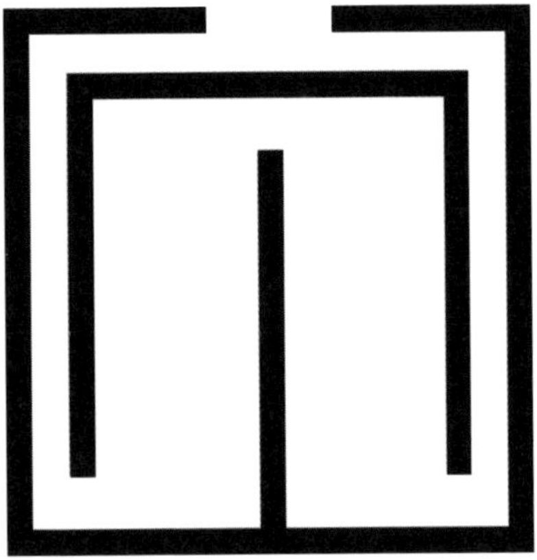

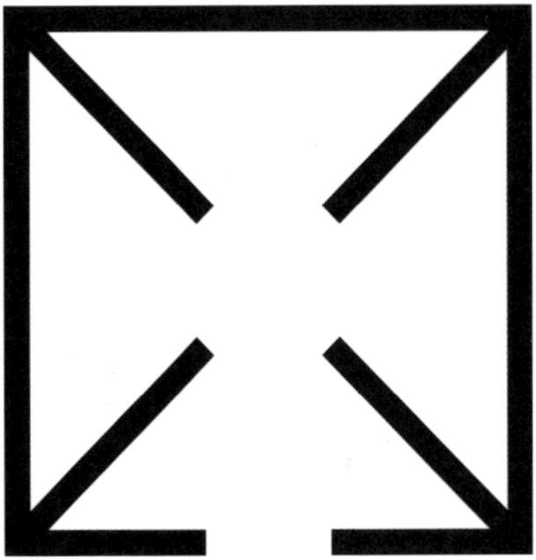

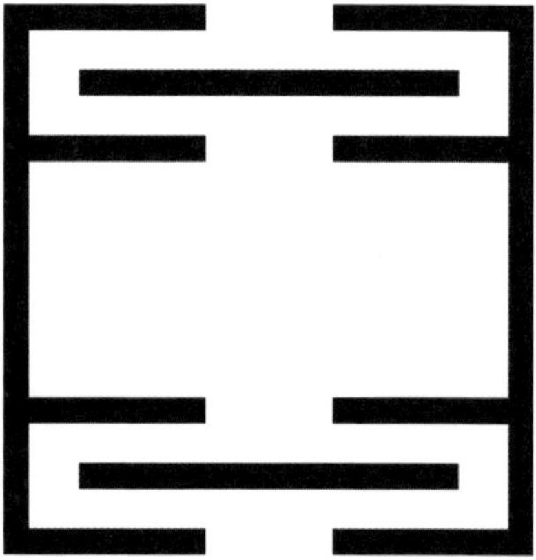

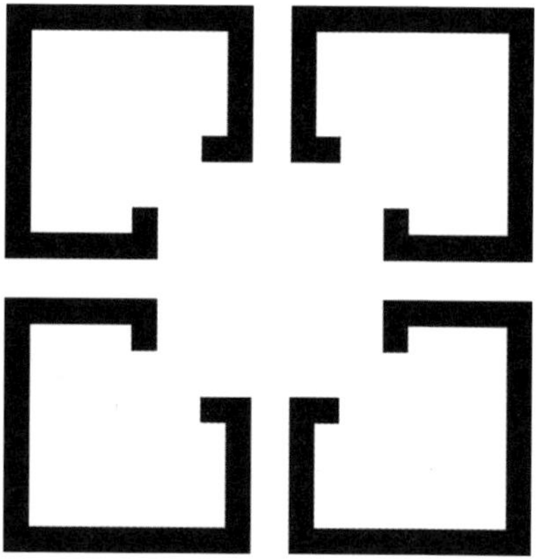

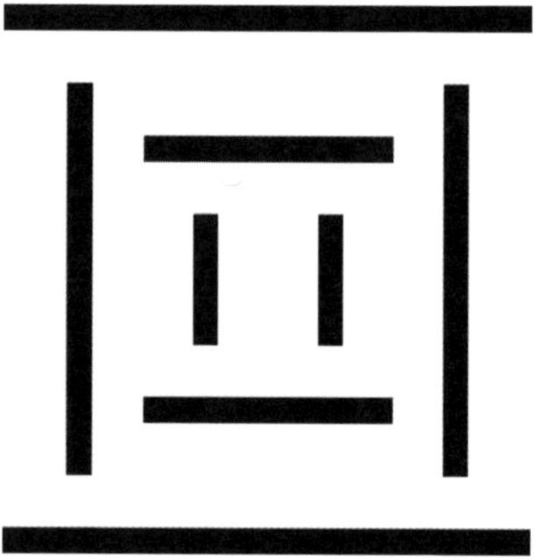

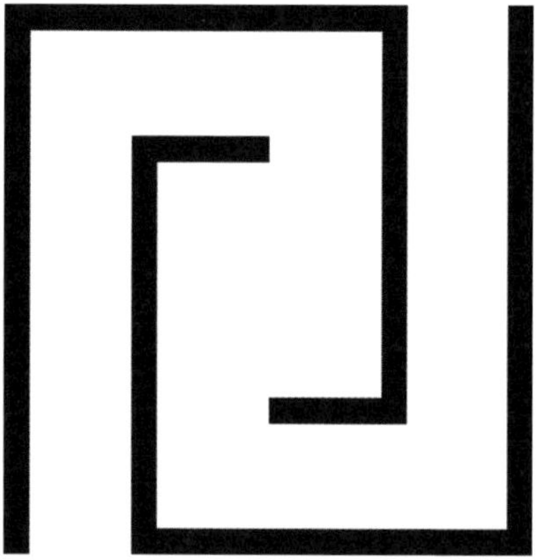

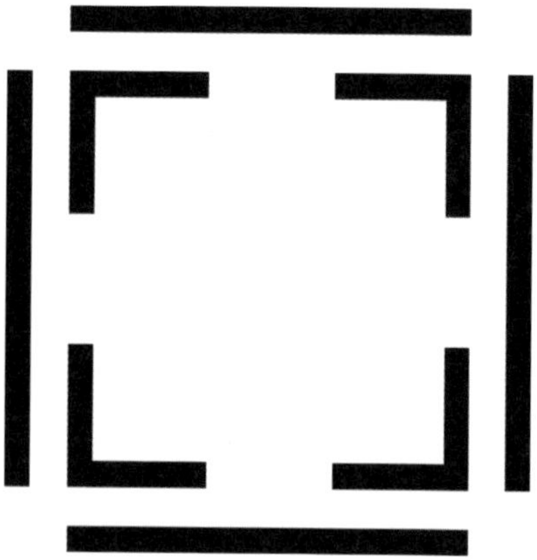

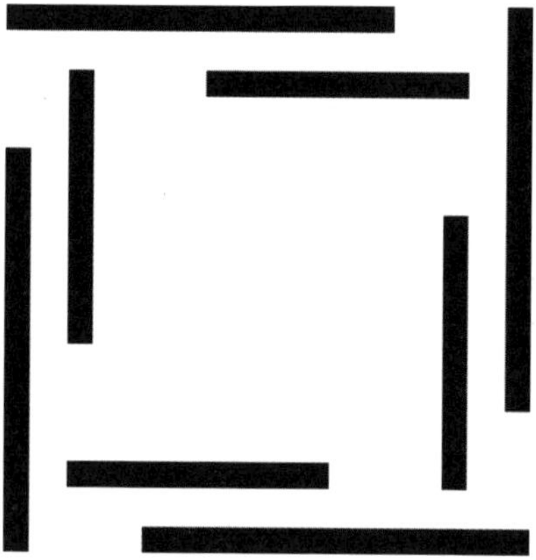

EPILOGUE

I can rouse a hundred forms
and fill them with spirit,
but when I look into your face,
I want to throw them in the fire.

Rumi

100 SERIES

As far as I can remember, I always had, and still have, a desire to classify, sort, and catalogue related things based on an established system, in order to look for correlations or variations in their apparent orders. In my formative years, I lent myself to these exercises on many occasions, where I repeatedly and methodically tried to make an inventory of the same object of a study. For example, I photographed all the people who were sleeping in an airport terminal or documented all the windows in a remote small village. Gradually, this led m to not just catalogue existing things but also create such collections myself both as open and closed series.

In 2012, I submitted myself to an exercise of drawing a different isometric cube every night for 100 consecutive days. The only mode of operation to create variations was subtraction. Later, I called this collection of 100 subtracted cubes *The Restless Cube*. Of course, I could have pushed this exercise and gone beyond one hundred iterations, to the point that it exhausts its main purpose and becomes redundant. But the number 100 is a magica figure that is large enough to prove its capacity beyond accidents but at the same time small enough to protect itself against exhaustion.

Since then, this exercise has become my obsession. I have pursued *100 Series* as an ongoing project, exploring serial works, taxonomies, typologies, and iterations as a means to explore possibilities, while remaining faithful to a set of predetermined rules, restrictions, and/or beliefs. The project intends to investigate the creative potential of a well-defined system to articulate a body of works with coherence. Sometimes, with more architectural themes, it proves to be freer both in thought and operation than working on a tabula rasa (freedom of context) or carte blanche (freedom of content).

By organizing a body of works around the method that originates them, designing does not end with a single project but continues through all projects, forming a genealogy, testifying to one big idea.

Now, at the age of fifty, with twenty-five series done, I am committed to making it all the way to one hundred 100 Series!

ACKNOWLEDGEMENT

To Actar Publishers, who once again took a chance on a not very conventional concept. It was a pleasure to collaborate with them on a sequel, they have been very accommodating.

Muchas gracias Ricardo por ser paciente con nosotros.

To everyone at Atelier RZLBD, without their efforts these little rooms would have never left my mind. Very special thanks go to:

James Chungwon Park	&	Katie Wang
Kam-sa Ham-ni-da.		*Xièxiè.*

It is no secret that being obsessed with what I do, I have often come short to give to my beloved ones. Now, at least I can dedicate a room to each one of them.

I welcome you to my many rooms.

_RZLBD, Summer 2023

AUTHOR'S BIOGRAPHY

Reza Aliabadi (RZLBD) is a Canadian artist and architect of Persian origin. He is the founder of Atelier RZLBD, an art and architecture practice based in Toronto, whose work extends to making arts, crafting objects, designing buildings, curating installations, and publishing a periodial zine called rzlbdPOST.

His work has been distinguished with numerous accolades including the International Architecture Master Prize (2018, 2019, 2020, 2021, 2022, 2023) American Architecture Prize (2017) and Ontario Association of Architects Awards (2009, 2011); exhibited in many venues including the Sir John Soane's Museum (London 2018) the World Architecture Festival (Berlin 2017, Amsterdam 2018) the School of Architecture at McGill University (Montreal 2009, 2017) and Toronto Harbourfront Centre (2012); and celebrated in more than one hundred print publications.

In 2017, RZLBD has been selected among the top emerging design talents in Canada. In the same year the UK publisher Artifice released a monograph, RZLBD HOPSCOTCH, which recognizes Reza's selected built projects by collecting essays, project profiles, and annotated drawings. In 2020, Actar published a pocket-sized manifesto, THE EMPTY ROOM, where Reza explores the idea of emptiness as the essence of architecture.

At the moment he divides his time between Toronto ON & Rochester NY, where he is appointed as the inaugural Vignelli Center Designer in Residence, to begin the conceptualization, planning, and determining the overall thematic direction of the RIT Outdoor Museum project.

100 Rooms

Reza Aliabadi, Atelier RZLBD
Toronto, Canada
www.rzlbd.com

Concept & Content
Atelier RZLBD

Graphic Design
Actar Publishers

Printing & Binding
Arlequin

Paper
Coral Book

Typeface
Adriane, Futura

Publisher
Actar Publishers
New York, Barcelona

www.actar.com

Distribution
Actar D, Inc. New York, Barcelona.

New York
440 Park Avenue South,
17th Floor
New York, NY 10016, USA
T +1 2129662207
salesnewyork@actar-d.com

Barcelona
Roca i Batlle 2-4
08023 Barcelona, Spain
T +34 933 282 183
eurosales@actar-d.com

Indexing
ISBN: 9781638401179
PCN: 2023948889
Printed in Barcelona, Spain